THE LISTENER

Alessandro Camon

BROADWAY PLAY PUBLISHING INC
New York
www.broadwayplaypublishing.com
info@broadwayplaypublishing.com

First edition: May 2024
I S B N: 979-8-88856-016-7

Book design: Marie Donovan
Page make-up: Adobe InDesign
Typeface: Palatino

CHARACTERS & SETTING

BETH, *a single woman in her 30s, living alone in a small house or apartment. She wears flannel plaid pajama bottoms and a sweatshirt. She's a helpline operator, working night shifts (the busy ones) from home.*
She is calm, empathetic, experienced at tuning into the caller's emotional register. Her voice is rich and soothing. She could have been a blues singer.
But mostly, of course: she listens.
She's a confessor who does not judge you, a confidant who won't gossip about you, the bartender who's heard a thousand stories, but will hear one more.
She wears ear pods, allowing her to move freely around her place.

The callers:

ANDY, *40s, blue collar, soon to be divorced*
MICHAEL, *40, recently released from prison*
CORINNE, *50s, stay-at-home-mom*
JINX, *19, unhoused, gender-fluid*
ELLIS, *20s, an incel*
SHARON, *30s, brilliant, mentally ill*
RAY, *45, Marine vet*
RUBY, *40, struggling actor*
MILTON, *70, retired, cognitively impaired*
CHRIS, *40, Sheriff's deputy*
LAURA, *40s, professor (laid off)*

*It will be possible for actors to play more than one role—
provided that voice and appearance change to clearly
represent a different character. All roles are open to all
ethnicities. Effort should be made to assemble a diverse cast
that reflects the community.*

There are a couple of ways to think about the staging:

One, BETH *and the callers could be located in their respective
settings.*

Two, the callers could inhabit BETH's *space, unseen by her,
like ghosts. Moving closer or further as needed, in a kind of
dance.*

*Director and actors are encouraged to develop the physical
behavior that will accompany each conversation.*

(BETH's *apartment*)

(*We hear an alarm ring. It stops.*)

(*Moments later, BETH turns on the lights, and we see the place. The furniture is mismatched, cobbled together from different times of her life, but the overall effect has a certain elegance. There are no family pictures, no special clues to her past, but there might be art on the wall, and a vase of flowers somewhere.*)

(*BETH moves to the kitchen area. Turns on the coffee machine. She walks to her desk, and turns on the computer. As the computer hums, she returns to the kitchen and pours coffee into the mug, adds some milk, then returns to the desk and puts on a headset. From this moment on:*)

(*She's working.*)

(*She will sometimes sit at her desk, sometimes move around the place. Stretching, pacing, drinking coffee, etc—but never, ever getting distracted.*)

(*BETH hits a key:*)

BETH: Hello. This is Beth.

(*The man on the other side of the call is ANDY. He's distressed. Trying to keep it together*)

ANDY: Oh, hi… Listen… Can you come out?

BETH: What do you mean?

ANDY: Can you come out here and talk to my wife?

BETH: Oh. Sorry…I can't come there, but if you put her on the phone—

ANDY: She's not gonna do that.

BETH: Are you sure? I can talk to both of you, together, or separately—whatever works for you. I just can't do it in person.
But if this is an emergency, I can give you—

ANDY: It's not that kind of emergency.

BETH: Okay… What's going on?

ANDY: I just told her I don't love her no more.

BETH: I see.

ANDY: Now I'm not sure what to do.

BETH: What did she say?

ANDY: She just went and locked herself in the bedroom.

BETH: Is she okay?

ANDY: What do you think?

BETH: Are you worried she might do something?

ANDY: No, I told you. It's not like that. She'd never…
We got kids.

BETH: Okay…

ANDY: I didn't want this, you know?
I don't even understand it…
What the fuck happened?
I loved her. Swear to god.
And then, one day, it was just… *gone*.
And you can't fucking… whistle for it.
You can't put up fliers on trees.
Once it's gone… Once you've said the words—
even just in your head—
once you admitted to yourself… Forget it.
It ain't coming back.

BETH: That's… not always true.

ANDY: It's not?

BETH: I mean, look…you'll have to do what's right for you…I'm just saying…sometimes it can come back.

ANDY: What, like a zombie?

(A sound of breaking glass)

ANDY: Shit…

BETH: What was that?

ANDY: I don't know… The mirror? She does that… She thinks it's about the other woman, so…

(Another object slams against a wall.)

ANDY: I should go check on her.

BETH: I think so.

ANDY: What do I say?

BETH: Maybe that you want to have an honest conversation. So that you can both understand where you are.
Just stay calm. No matter what.
Don't raise your voice, don't escalate.

ANDY: Alright…

BETH: Call me back anytime, okay?

ANDY: Yeah… If I fucking live.
(He hangs up.)

*(*BETH *sips coffee. She stares at a pack of cigarettes, then sticks it in a drawer. She takes the next call:* MICHAEL. *He's high-energy, extroverted, upbeat. But there's a sense it could all crash any moment.)*

MICHAEL: Hi.

BETH: How are you tonight?

MICHAEL: Yeah, good. I'm fine.

BETH: Good. No sleep?

MICHAEL: Yeah, some nights I just…
I was in prison for a while.
Never really went back to normal.

BETH: I get it.

MICHAEL: At first I was sleeping *a lot*. Too much
stimulation. I was like a puppy at the dog park.
Soon as I got home, I just needed to sleep.

BETH: I can imagine.

MICHAEL: And then after a while I started staying up
late—but I still got up early.
Until the 'rona went off.
After that, it was just, whatever.

BETH: I remember well.

MICHAEL: It wasn't all bad. In some ways, it helped.

BETH: Did it?

MICHAEL: Yeah… In prison, they got these transition
units. They give you a little bit more freedom, a little
bit at a time, so you start getting used to it.
But I didn't go through that.
I went straight from the SHU to the street.
So it's probably good I got some time to adjust.
Wasn't hard for me to stay home, you know?
Everyone was bitchin' so much about it…
I was like, bro: You tellin' me I can eat when I want,
sleep when I want, wear what I want?
That's supposed to be hard?

BETH: That's funny. I don't mean funny—I mean—
MICHAEL: No, it *was* funny…
I was sitting with my grandma one night…
She said, Michael, it's so weird—the day's so slow…
But then, at the end, feels like it lasted a minute.
I told her—that's *prison* time.
Day's slow because nothing happens.

And when it's gone, feels like it never even started.
You don't even remember nothing,
Because *nothing happened.*

BETH: Wow… That's deep.

MICHAEL: Know what was weird though?

BETH: What's that?

MICHAEL: Wearing a mask in a store.
I mean, I couldn't even get a mask…
First time, I had to use this bandana my sister gave me.
I was like, I don't know about this…
Last time I entered a store with a bandana on, I got
shot. Shot *and* arrested.
She was like, never mind that—
now they won't let you in *without* a mask.
So I go shopping, with this bandana on…
And I mean, I always have this feeling
that people check me out,
like they can tell I've been inside…

BETH: That's probably in your mind, though…

MICHAEL: It isn't. Trust me. I mean, I can tell in two
seconds if a guy's been inside.

BETH: Really.

MICHAEL: Hell, yeah. It's the way you carry yourself…
Like, you don't want anyone too close.
Stay out of my space, I'll stay out of yours.
It's an awareness—you know?
And *respect.*
It's like animals in the wild.
You don't know what's coming from behind that rock.

BETH: That makes sense.

MICHAEL: So, *I know* people can tell.
Even if they don't know what it is, exactly?
They can tell there's something different about me.

It's like they can smell it.
I don't mean literally. I smell real nice these days…
Believe that.

BETH: I believe it.

MICHAEL: Anyway—so I'm already stressing out about being around people…Now I gotta wear a bandana, like I'm robbing the place…
The guy at the cash register, I'm thinking—
He's gonna pull a shotgun any second.
I start sweating. My heartbeat's up.
So if he didn't think I was suspicious, he sure as hell thinks it now.
I take my stuff to the counter, he rings me up, and he goes: Did you find everything you were looking for?
And I'm like, *What?* Like I don't understand the question.
Which I didn't, cause I'm spaced out, and I got a fucking bandana on, and I'm not even used to hearing this kind of question—I'm used to hearing, Move along, or some shit.
So he repeats the question, and I'm like, Yessir.
And then I skip a beat and I go, *Thanks.*
And I know he's thinking, What's wrong with this dude?
So I pay, and I gotta hand him cash. I don't have no credit card.
And I see he's watching the tattoo on my hand…
I'm gonna get it removed, but I haven't got around to it yet.
I don't know—I guess it's still a part of me…
Like, I'm not proud of it? But this is who I am.

BETH: And then what happened?

MICHAEL: Nothing. He said, Have a good night.
And then I walk out, and I realize, Damn. No…
I didn't find everything I was looking for.

I was in such a rush to get out of there, I forgot half of
it.

BETH: That happens to me all the time…

MICHAEL: Yeah?

BETH: Oh, yeah. Unless I have a written list?
I'm always gonna forget something.
I can't retain that kind of information.

(A beat)

MICHAEL: I got used to it, though. The mask, I mean.

BETH: That's good.

MICHAEL: I was like, Okay…people can think whatever
they want.
They can't see me. I don't care what they think.

BETH: Right.

(A longer beat)

MICHAEL: I'm not a bad person.

BETH: I know.

MICHAEL: How do you know?

BETH: Oh, I guess…I mean…
I don't have any reason to think otherwise.

MICHAEL: I just never had a chance.
My father went down when I was six.
He just died three years ago.

BETH: Sorry to hear that.

MICHAEL: It's okay. We never really had a relationship.
I was raised by my grandma.
My mom, after he got arrested, she said to me:
I can handle your sisters—*you?*
You gotta move in with your grandma.
Shipped me off like a package…

BETH: That's rough… You were six?

MICHAEL: Just about to start school.
I hated it…
I was this broke little punk with no father, living with
an old lady…
I didn't have any friends.
I walked back home alone every day.
After a month, I started taking a different way…
I cut through this alley, where the homeboys hung out.
They started joking with me, making me laugh…
That's when I started noticing stuff.

BETH: What do you mean? What stuff?

MICHAEL: Like, the tattoos… The graffiti.
I mean, I'd been seeing them my whole life…
but I never really paid attention. It was just paint.
And now it was like…they were speaking to me.
Like I finally understood the language.
That was my path to prison right there.

BETH: Wow. I just saw the whole picture.
Thanks for that.

MICHAEL: You're welcome.

BETH: So…is there anything you need?
Anything I can help you with?

MICHAEL: I don't know. I'm a little bit worried, I guess.

BETH: About what?

MICHAEL: I mean…I don't have any money.
Had this job at an auto glass repair…
They went out of business.
Wasn't the greatest job in the world, but…

BETH: Have you been looking? For another job?

MICHAEL: Yeah, sure… It's tough out there.
I don't have a lot of skills.
I'm a good tattoo artist—like, I could do that for a
living, but…

BETH: Nothing wrong with that.

MICHAEL: I know, but it's not easy to make money.
Plus, unless you're in some fancy shop,
Half your customers are gonna be trouble…
Parole officer would be all over me.

BETH: I understand.

MICHAEL: So, I don't know. I don't know how I'm
gonna make rent.
Never mind that I need dental work.
I've been living on soup and Orajel…

BETH: I can give you a number for financial assistance,
if—

MICHAEL: I'm already doing all that.

BETH: Okay…

MICHAEL: Hey—worse comes to worse…
I still got my bandana, right?
That was a joke.

BETH: I know.

MICHAEL: You're not tracing these calls, are you?

BETH: No worries. There's no tracing, not recording…
I'm just sitting here at home talking to you.

MICHAEL: You're at home?

BETH: Yeah… Some helplines have to use offices,
but we're set up to take calls from home.

MICHAEL: That's cool.

BETH: Listen… I think you should check out this
group—
It's called Hand Up. You know, as opposed to handout.
It's run by formerly incarcerated people—
they can help with jobs, housing, everything…

MICHAEL: Is one of the guys named Jackson?

BETH: That I don't know.
Let me give you the number—

MICHAEL: That's alright. I'll find it.

BETH: Okay…

MICHAEL: I just needed to talk.

BETH: Anytime.

MICHAEL: That was a joke about the bandana, okay?
I'm not gonna rob nobody.

BETH: I kn—

(MICHAEL *hangs up.* BETH *refills her mug, then turns the machine off. She goes back to the computer and takes the next call. It's* CORINNE. *She speaks softly.*)

BETH: Hello, this is Beth.

CORINNE: Hi.

BETH: How are you doing tonight?

CORINNE: Like always, I guess…

BETH: Is that good?

CORINNE: You know… Okay—you know when someone says something annoying…like really annoying, or even hurtful, and you just suck it up, then you go home and replay the moment in your head, and come up with the perfect comeback? The exact thing you should have said?

BETH: Oh, yeah…

CORINNE: Well… That's my life. A day late, and a dollar short.

BETH: Hey, we all feel like that sometimes.

CORINNE: Yeah, well—I feel like that all the time.
Besides—I don't think it's it true.
I don't think Oprah feels like that.
Or Jeff Zuckerberg.

(BETH *notices the mix-up, smiles, but doesn't correct*
CORINNE.)

BETH: Maybe not… Certainly not the "dollar short"
part.

CORINNE: Right? What d'you even do with all that
money?
Meanwhile, my husband got his hours cut.
And I'm cutting coupons.

BETH: That's rough…

CORINNE: Our daughter has special needs.
I'm a full-time support system.
Can't even take a break. *Ever.*
If I got sick…I don't even wanna think about it.
What's gonna happen to her when I'm gone. I just
can't…
(She starts crying.)
I'm sorry.

BETH: It's absolutely fine.

CORINNE: I don't usually do this…

BETH: It's okay… Let it all out. This is what I'm here
for.

CORINNE: Can I call you back?

BETH: Anytime. Ask for Beth.

(CORINNE *hangs up.* BETH *takes a long breath, then takes
the next call. It's* JINX.)

BETH: Hello.

JINX: Hello?

BETH: Hi, there.

JINX: You sound old.

BETH: I'm not so young, I guess.
You sound young.

JINX: Just turned nineteen.

BETH: Happy birthday.

JINX: I hate birthdays.

BETH: Wait till you get to my age…

JINX: Yeah, that's not gonna happen.

BETH: Why do you say that?

JINX: Whatever. I just never had a good birthday.
Except five years ago, I guess… When I run away.
That was my birthday present to myself.

BETH: Where do you live now?

JINX: A cozy two-person tent.

BETH: I see. You have a case worker?

JINX: Not anymore… My boyfriend fell out with him.
He's such an asshole…

BETH: How long have you two been together?

JINX: Since I left home.

BETH: You met on the street?

JINX: Yeah. I'd left town with a friend, but she
chickened out after two nights.
So I hooked up with these guys.
They had guitars, and weed. And a dog.
I loved that dog…
He died last month.

BETH: I'm sorry.

JINX: Dustin's not doing great, either.

BETH: Dustin's your boyfriend?

JINX: For lack of a better word.

BETH: What's wrong with him?

JINX: I don't know…I think he's got hep or something.

BETH: Did he go to a doctor?

JINX: Yeah, right. He's totally paranoid about doctors.
I'm not even gonna ask. He flips out.
He's got like major anger issues.

BETH: That's not good.

JINX: I told you. He's a fucking asshole.
He thinks that I should make him money now.

BETH: What do you mean?

JINX: He wants to be my fucking pimp. Fuck that shit…

BETH: Where's Dustin right now?

JINX: I don't know… Hanging with his buddies
somewhere.

BETH: Sounds like maybe you shouldn't be seeing this
guy.

JINX: Yeah, no shit.

BETH: So…

JINX: It's not so simple.

BETH: Why not?

JINX: It's just not… You think I want to be alone out
here?
You think I can go on fucking Homeless Tinder,
Find myself a better dude?
Plus, it's not like I don't have issues…

BETH: Alright, look… Let me give you a number for
Social Services.
I'll give you this guy's direct line—he's the best…

JINX: Oh, shit…

BETH: What?

JINX: I think he's back…
Yep, that's him.

He's coming up the street.
I gotta go—if he hears I'm talking to you…

BETH: Can you write down this number?

JINX: Shit. He's fucking wasted.

BETH: Here's the number:

JINX: I'll call you back.

BETH: Are you gonna be okay?

JINX: Nope.

(The line breaks.)

*(*BETH *closes her eyes, takes a few long breaths. She reopens her eyes, takes in her familiar surroundings. She takes the next call:* ELLIS. *Dripping sarcasm)*

BETH: Hi. This is Beth.

ELLIS: Beth? That your real name?

BETH: Actually, we are not allowed to use real names.

ELLIS: That's what I thought. Call me Kratos, then.
Call me fucking… Solid Snake.

BETH: That might be a little awkward, don't you think?

ELLIS: Whatever. Call me whatever you want.
You can call me Ellis—that's my real name.

BETH: How are you tonight?

ELLIS: Great. Fantastic. That's obviously why I'm
calling, right?

BETH: I suppose not.
Wanna talk about it?
(Silence)
You don't have to.

ELLIS: I've just fucking had it. I'm so *done* with it.

BETH: With what?

ELLIS: Just…the rejection. The contempt.

BETH: From whom?
Women?

ELLIS: You think I'm a freak, don't you?

BETH: I don't. I wouldn't. I just met you.

ELLIS: I've been dealing with this shit my whole life…

BETH: I understand.

ELLIS: No, you don't. You *don't* understand. You can't.
'Cause you're not wired that way. Genetically
programmed to need something you can't have. It's
like…I don't even know how to explain it. It's fucked
up. You can't *not* need it. Nature makes you need it.
Society—it tells you must have it. And then you're
denied. Rejected. Over. And over. And over.
So the only choice you have, is whether to hate
yourself, or hate them.
All the fucking guys who ever made you feel like a
piece of shit.
All the girls who mocked you, avoided you, looked
right through you. Like you were nothing. And threw
themselves at those idiots, who just happened to have
the right look, the fucking jacket, the fucking car, the
fucking hair…
Course, you always end up hating both.
Yourself, *and* them.

BETH: Maybe hate isn't the right way to—

ELLIS: You don't think I tried the other way?
Samantha fucking Robinson…
I would have bled for her. I would have taken a bullet.
And she made me watch.
She kissed that asshole right in front of me,
Knowing I was watching. Knowing how I felt…
I had my revenge, though…
I found this porno… The girl had the same exact body.

I deep-faked Samantha's face on it, sent it to everyone.
She had to move to a different school.
You judge me yet? Go ahead, tell me.

BETH: I…don't like the action you described.

ELLIS: Yeah, well…it's not the worst thing I've done.
I made another film…
Pulled two hours' worth of accident footage
from CCTV cameras all around the world…
Only the goriest shit.
I mean, sick as fuck. Splattered children.
I cut it together to Disney music, And I put it on three
hundred school websites.
People went nuts!
(He laughs, then stops abruptly.)
I don't expect you to understand.
Maybe if you had to endure all the rejection I've had…
If you were a man who's not allowed to feel like a man.
Too short, too soft, too chubby…
Whatever society has deemed inadequate about you.
Too little hair on your head.
Too broke to buy nice clothes.
But you can't even imagine, can you?
What do you even look like?

BETH: What do I look like?

ELLIS: That's what I asked.

BETH: Just…average.

ELLIS: That's not very informative.
What—are you too shy?
I don't care if you're chubby. I mean, I'm hideous.
I bet you're not, though.

BETH: I'm sorry. I don't want to talk about that.

ELLIS: I thought the whole point of this line was to talk
to real people.

BETH: That's right.

ELLIS: So? Be real.
Can you even relate to anything that I'm saying?

BETH: Sure…I was a misfit. I didn't have nice clothes.

ELLIS: Your family was broke?

BETH: I wouldn't say broke… But struggling.

ELLIS: You had your assets though.
You could trade on looks.
Don't lie to me… You were good-looking.
I can tell from your voice.
You probably still are. Am I right?

BETH: I'm not comfortable talking about that.

ELLIS: Why? Did I freak you out when I mentioned
porn? I don't even watch porn anymore. It's too
freakin' painful. Just a constant reminder that twenty
gets eighty.

BETH: *(Confused)* What's that?

ELLIS: Oh, that's like…basic science.
Twenty percent of men have eighty percent of all sex.

BETH: I'm not sure what that means.

ELLIS: Means that out of any ten women who are
providing sex, eight of them provide it to the same
two guys. The Alphas. The Chads. So the other eighty
percent of men, Beta to Omega, they're left fighting
for twenty percent of females. The cast-offs. And of
course, not only do that twenty percent of women have
this huge eighty percent pool of men to choose from…
Most of the time they're not even looking! 'Cause
they're not designed to need sex nearly as much as
men.
Anyone who says otherwise is just full of shit, by the
way.
Long story short: if you're at the bottom of the male

percentage?
A fucking Omega?
Forget it. No chance.
Best you can expect is to be friend-zoned, where you
have to pretend you believe all the feminist stuff.
Pretend you don't want sex in return for being nice.
And anyone who says that is *really* full of shit.

BETH: Where do you get all this?

ELLIS: I read the books, lady.

BETH: What books?

ELLIS: The ones they don't tell you about in school.
It all works, by the way. I've seen it work.
It just doesn't work for everybody.
Some of us, even with the knowledge…
we're just fucked.

BETH: Maybe…it's about adjusting expectations.

ELLIS: Yeah, no. This isn't about my standards.
I'd go with a Becky—*Becky* thinks she's too good for
me.
(He mumbles something we don't quite hear.)

BETH: I'm sorry?

ELLIS: I'm just tired of it… Going through life like
this…evolutionary failure. This unloved, unwanted
piece of shit.

BETH: Alright, listen…you can't think like that.
I promise you, you will feel different at some point.
May I ask you what you do for a living?

ELLIS: I work in IT. I used to be a content moderator.
You know what that is?

BETH: Sort of. I guess.

ELLIS: Basically you sit at the computer, and screen out
all the sick shit people post.
I did it for about a year.

Then they accused me of posting sick shit myself…
I guess they didn't get the joke.
So, now I just fix network shit.

BETH: Well…okay. So, you're smart.

ELLIS: What's your point?

BETH: My point is, that's a very big asset.
I think the anger works against you. But you can
change that.

ELLIS: Backtrack. Say the first part again.

BETH: What do you mean?

ELLIS: After You're smart—what did you say?

BETH: I said, that's very good.

ELLIS: No, that's not what you said.
Just say it like you said it before.

BETH: I don't understand.

ELLIS: Will you please just repeat *exactly* what you said?

BETH: I think I said, That's a very big asset.

ELLIS: Okay… Yes. That was it.
Keep talking.

BETH: Look…you're in a cloud right now. But the cloud
will pass.

ELLIS: You have a nice voice.

BETH: Thank you.

ELLIS: Keep talking.

BETH: What else can I tell you?

ELLIS: What…what are you wearing right now?

BETH: Oh… Sorry—I'm not playing that game.

ELLIS: Just say that thing again.

BETH: I don't think so.

ELLIS: Okay, just… Just breathe then. Please?
Just breathe into the receiver for me?

(BETH *remains silent.*)

ELLIS: One fucking breath…
You're not gonna give me one fucking breath!?

BETH: Have a good night.

ELLIS: Yeah—fuck you too.

(BETH *and* ELLIS *both hang up. She gives herself a moment.*)

(*Next up:* SHARON. *She talks fast.*)

SHARON: Hello?

BETH: Hello, there. I'm Beth.

SHARON: I'm mentally ill. Let's get that out of the way,
right? I'm mental. So, there you go.
I used to hate that word… Now I'm like, fuck it.
It's a cool word. *Mental.* Cool, like cigarettes.

BETH: When you say mental…

SHARON: Borderline and bipolar. Psychotic episodes.
Mainly I'm just on edge.
Kinda like, if you're alone in a dark parking structure?
And you just have this feeling you shouldn't be there?
That something bad's about to happen?
Like that.

BETH: I see.

SHARON: I have it right now. I'm at home, and I have a
feeling I shouldn't be here.
I'm probably talking too fast, right?
That's the other thing. The words just roll out.

BETH: Are you taking medication?

SHARON: Do you know anything about magnetrons?

BETH: What?

SHARON: The thingies inside microwaves.
I just warmed up a plate and I left the spoon in, And
the microwave got all sparky. I think I might have
damaged the magnetron.
They have beryllium inside.
Which if you inhale even a tiny speck, you're *done.*
It's like, weapons-grade shit.

BETH: I'm afraid I don't know anything about it…
I don't use the microwave very much.

SHARON: Gas can be dangerous too, you know.
A slow leak, you won't even smell it.

BETH: That's true…

SHARON: I'm not taking anything.

BETH: Oh. How come?

SHARON: I lost my health insurance. It's with the socks
now…

BETH: I'm sorry?

SHARON: You, know, when you lose a sock? Just one
sock. The other is still there. But one sock every six
pairs or so, always disappears, right? Doesn't matter
where you live—small place, big place… Doesn't
matter what kind of sock—short, long, white, colors.
There's a place socks just like to go.
Maybe that's where all lost things go, you know?
All the shit people lose all day long…
The signal. The opportunity. Sleep. Patience. Control…
whatever.
Maybe it's all there. With the socks.
I liked this guy once… He was a comedian.
I thought he was funny.
But then one day he bombed, and he never went on
stage again.
He said he lost his mojo.
He became depressed, and he couldn't deal with my

shit anymore.
And that was it — he lost his mojo, and I lost him.
I bet he's wearing my socks now.
I bet he got fat.
I lost ten pounds. I bet he found them.

BETH: When did you lose your insurance?

SHARON: Six months ago? Maybe seven.

BETH: So… are you not seeing a doctor?

SHARON: Oh, yeah…I'm sure. Whenever I go out,
there's probably a doctor somewhere.

BETH: I meant—

SHARON: Kidding! No. I was for a while, but he moved
out of state.
So, no meds, no doctor, no insurance.
Welcome to America, right?

BETH: I hear you.

SHARON: I didn't much like him, to tell you the truth.

BETH: I can put you in touch—

SHARON: Uh-uh. Don't *even*. I'm not in the fucking
mood for that shit.
Last thing I need is to be sent to some shitty hospital
with shitty nurses who just look down on you.
They don't help you. All they do is fill forms and talk
shit behind your back.
And then they bill you for it.

BETH: I understand. Maybe we could—

SHARON: I feel weird.

BETH: How so?

SHARON: I feel like my bones have turned to snakes.

BETH: What do you mean?

SHARON: I mean, I have snakes for bones. They make my body move funny.
I think I'm having an episode.
Knock knock.

BETH: Who's there?

SHARON: I have no fucking idea.

BETH: Okay… Listen—I'll stay on the phone.
I'll be right here with you, but maybe we should—

SHARON: You know, I don't hear voices.

Everybody always asks that… No. I don't.
I *see* them.

BETH: See them?

SHARON: Like, your voice—I can see it right now. It's blue.
Got a little green in it.
I can smell it, too…
I can smell you through the phone.
You smell nice. Like a fluffy cloud.
(Laughs)
Got you there, didn't I?

BETH: You sure did…

SHARON: Seriously, though. I can.
Do you believe me?

BETH: I'm…confused now.

SHARON: There you go! Get it?

BETH: Get what?

SHARON: That's how it works!
You don't know *what* to believe.
Except it's all in your own head.
Like, you don't know when you can believe yourself.

BETH: But they do have meds for that…

SHARON: I don't do well with meds!
I can't moderate.
Either I don't take 'em, or I take the whole bottle.
They're all shit, anyway. They don't work.
If they work, they make you lethargic.
You don't ever want to have sex again.
Drugs are a lie.
They just want you on drugs so you don't know anything.
You don't care about anything.
All the shit happening in the world…
New viruses.
Computer bugs.
They spy on you.
And no one cares.
Secret prisons
Child porn
Killer hornets
Killer clowns
Ethnic cleansing
Leaky implants
Honor killings
Over-billing
Toxic sludge
Man on ledge—
No one cares!
No one cares.

BETH: Wow…

SHARON: I'm sorry…
Brian goes off like that, sometimes.

BETH: Brian?

SHARON: That's what I call my brain. Brian.
Cause it's scrambled.
I'm not even talking right now.
I'm not the one talking.

The thoughts have their own mind.
They talk right through me.
I can read your thoughts.
I can read the fine print.
But the thoughts that come out of my mouth—
I don't know them until they're out.

BETH: That…must be tough.

SHARON: Yeah, well…I can't play society's game.
That's for sure.
Whenever someone tries that shit on me,
Brian's just like, fuck you—I *will* look in the horse's mouth.
I *will* make mountains out of molehills.
I will catch a falling knife,
I will take that knife to the gunfight,
and I will cut my nose to spite my face.
How about that?
And I will cross that fucking bridge before I get to it.
That's how I roll, baby.

(BETH *takes that in.*)

SHARON: What?

BETH: I didn't say anything.

SHARON: I can smell it.

BETH: I'm just thinking… You know you have a gift, right?

SHARON: A *gift?*

BETH: I mean…you're kind of a poet.
The way your mind makes connections…
I don't know—maybe you're imagining things,
but isn't that's what poetry does?
Just kind of look at things sideways, or…differently.
I don't know. I don't mean to romanticize it.
I just think you're talented.

(A moment passes.)

SHARON: I like rap.

BETH: Yeah? You should write some lyrics.

SHARON: Like a song?

BETH: A song, or a poem…whatever comes.

SHARON: Okay. I'm gonna go now.

(And just like that, SHARON *hangs up.* BETH *takes a moment to process, then takes the next call. It's* RAY. *He's a little drunk [but lucid].)*

BETH: Hello, this is Beth.

RAY: Yeah, hi…I'm Ray.

BETH: Nice to meet you, Ray. How are you tonight?

RAY: How am I? Well…let's see…
had a few drinks before I went to sleep…
Then I had a fucking nightmare…
So, now I'm having another drink.

BETH: Wanna talk about it?

RAY: What? The drink?
Or the nightmare?

BETH: Either. Both.

RAY: Drink is scotch. Nightmare is… A boot.

BETH: A boot?

RAY: Yeah.

BETH: Like a cowboy boot?

RAY: Military.

BETH: Are you in the Army?

RAY: Nah. Marines. *Was.*
I don't like to call the Vet lines, if that's what you're about to suggest.

BETH: It's fine.

RAY: They just follow their scripts.
Makes you feel like you're talking to what's her name.
The robot lady.

BETH: Siri?

RAY: That's right.

BETH: You are always welcome to call this line.

RAY: You sound like this Officer I knew…
Captain Berger.
She was tough.
Once she overheard a dude call her a Marinette…
Put him on latrine duty for a month.
She was cool with me, though.

BETH: Where was that?

RAY: Afghanistan. Hindu Kush.
(Sing-song)
Hindu Kush, Hindu Kush,
Baby I dream of your tush
Taliban, you fucking douche
Gonna kill you for President Bush

BETH: That's catchy.

RAY: Hey, what d'you call an Afghan who owns a
camel and a goat?

BETH: What?

RAY: Bisexual.
(Laughs)
I know, I know…that's racist.
What can I say. War zones ain't safe zones.

BETH: So…what's up with the boot?

RAY: That was Iraq.
Afghanistan, I came back without a scratch.
Iraq… That's where I got messed up.
Was about three months in the first time I got shot…

BETH: What happened?

RAY: I don't really remember it…
I was in this house, someone shot me, I fell down a
stairwell.
That's what they told me.
Ended up in the hospital, then back home…
Didn't feel like home though. Not anymore.

BETH: How do you mean?

RAY: It's funny, you missed your bed so much…
And now you're in your bed, and it's dead quiet…
And you can't sleep for shit.
Try to explain that to the missus.
How much you miss sleeping in a room full of dudes
and guns.
(He drinks.)
The war was bullshit.
Twenty years in Afghanistan,
Four Presidents, two trillion dollars,
Hundreds of thousands killed…
All to replace the Taliban with the Taliban.
All that crap about hearts and minds—
none of it meant a fucking thing.
Your buddies… That's the only thing.
Only thing that meant something.
Cuz each and everyone of them would have died for
you, Just like you would for them.
And then you're back…
Homeless people everywhere—and many of them
served…
No one gives a fuck.
Everybody just drives by,
yakking on the phone.

BETH: Want to tell me about the boot?

RAY: Right. The boot…
After I recovered, I got redeployed.

One night, we drove to this farm…
We were supposed to arrest two guys.
The whole place was booby-trapped.
Rodriguez got blown up.
Finally we start clearing the buildings.
I'm pretty jumpy, so when I see this guy come out of
nowhere…
I just squeeze the trigger.
It was a forty year old woman.
She had five children.

(BETH *takes that in.*)

RAY: All I wanted was to be a Jedi.

BETH: I'm sorry?

RAY: Sure, you want to help your country, yadda
yadda.
And you want the paycheck.
But honestly? I just wanted to learn stuff.
Secret stuff.
I wanted to be that guy in the bar.
The guy with the cool tattoos, and the cool stories.
Guess what I learned?

BETH: What's that?

RAY: I learned what bodies smell like
after they've been in the sun three days.
I can look at someone on the street—
I know what they'd look like dead.
What do you do with that kind of knowledge?
I killed four guys.
I think.
One of them, I can't be sure.
So, maybe just three.
I'm sure they were combatants.
But then there was her.
They don't teach you how to live with that.

BETH: I'm sorry…

RAY: I came back, they had this big welcome party…
People buying me beers, calling me a hero.
No one ever mentioned her again.
The report cleared me, no further question—
Everything is forgiven.
'Cept you sit alone at night…

(A beat)

BETH: So…what about the boot?

RAY: Right… So, basically, ten minutes after I killed
her, I stepped onto an IED.
I was lucky. I mean, compared to Manny.
Bomb just took my foot clean off.
Boot and all.
No one could find it.

BETH: Jesus… Didn't see that coming.

RAY: Yeah… Me neither.
Anyway—in the dream, she brings me my boot.
I think I need some Advil.
Thanks for your time.

BETH: Wait… Can I ask you a question?

RAY: Shoot.

BETH: I mean, if she's just bringing you your boot…
Why is it a nightmare?

RAY: Cuz up to that point I have both feet.
When she holds up the boot…
That's when I realize my foot is gone.

BETH: Huh.
You know…us modern people…
We think that dreams are about stuff that happened.
The ancients—they thought dreams were about the
future.
Like prophecies, or…advice.

RAY: What are you saying?

BETH: Well, I'm no shrink, but…I don't know. *A boot?*

RAY: What about it?

BETH: You're still stuck there. In your heart. You're still there.

RAY: No shit.

BETH: Maybe she's telling you can walk away.

(A beat)

RAY: You think so?

BETH: I do.

RAY: Well…*shit.*
I'm gonna have to think about that.

BETH: Good.
Why don't you try to get some sleep now?

RAY: Yeah… Good idea.
Goodnight, then.

BETH: Goodnight.

(BETH and RAY hang up. She checks her watch. She takes off her headset, stretches, then puts her headset back on and takes the next call. LAURA. Cloaked in shadow.)

BETH: Hello, this is Beth.

(No answer. Just the faint sound of classical music in the background.)

BETH: Hello, this is Beth…
How are you tonight?
Take your time…
Whenever you're ready.

(Nothing happens.)

BETH: I know this can be difficult.

(And now LAURA *hangs up.* BETH *sighs. Shakes her head. Next call:* RUBY. *She's chirpy. Probably high)*

BETH: Hello.

RUBY: Hey there…I'm Ruby.

BETH: Hi, Ruby. I'm Beth.

RUBY: No, you're not… It's a stage name, isn't it?

BETH: Well…I wouldn't call it a stage name, but…

RUBY: That's okay. Mine is too.

BETH: I see.

RUBY: My agent didn't think Virginia would work…
I hated Virginia, anyway.
Ruby didn't work either, though.
So, in my head, I don't even have a name now.
Virginia's dead…Ruby never really existed.
She was meant to be famous, but she just failed.
And no one fails like an actor fails…
A failed actor must fail tragically, *and* comically.
Because she must think all along that failure is a test.
She must be in denial.
How else would you endure years of auditions?
Broken promises, backstabbing, fair-weather friends…
Cause that's what it is. That's show business for you.
And everybody just plays along.
They all see everyone else for what they are.
Wannabes. Posers. Name droppers.
Fucking…crevice dwellers.
But they all tell themselves, You're different.
You're the one with the talent.
Well, I'm done. Had my last fucking humiliation.

BETH: I'm sorry.

RUBY: It was classic… Get this—I auditioned for a student film.
That's right—*auditioned.*

For *a student film.*
And I didn't get it.
I don't even know how I lasted this long…
I hate them all so much! The sharks, the liars…
The suckers who fall for them.
Taking selfies on the red carpet.
So fucking desperate…
So thirsty to sneak backstage, into the VIP room, the
secret party, where it will finally happen, some famous
someone will discover them, And everything will
change…
Driving around with their motivational tapes on,
Going to sleep with their meditation apps,
And saving up for the botox…
And the more the dream fades,
the more desperate they get to maintain the illusion…
To look good, to stay fit, to score the invitation.
To get the fucking *likes.*
And the whole town's in on it.
Every liar and lawyer and publicist and therapist
And plastic surgeon and drug dealer
And dreamer and schemer…
So fucking pathetic.
I'm a mess, aren't I?
Fuck it… Goodnight.

(RUBY *hangs up.* BETH *smiles.*)

(*Next:* MILTON. *He sounds confused.*)

BETH: Hello. This is Beth.

MILTON: Angela?

BETH: Beth.

MILTON: Where's Angela?

BETH: I… don't know an Angela.

Did you ask for Angela at the switchboard?

MILTON: What?

BETH: When you called, did you ask for Angela?

MILTON: You're not with Angela?

BETH: I'm not.

MILTON: Fuck… What are you wasting my time for?
(He hangs up.)

BETH: Nice.

(Next call. CHRIS. *Sharp-edged)*

BETH: Hi.

CHRIS: Hello. What do I call you?

BETH: You can call me Beth.

CHRIS: Alright. You can call me Chris.

BETH: Good to meet you, Chris.

CHRIS: You hate cops?

BETH: No.

CHRIS: 'Cause a lot of people do these days.

BETH: Are you a cop?

CHRIS: Yeah. Sheriff's deputy.
That's kinda what I'm calling about.
We have psychologists—
I just don't wanna be seen anywhere near them.
Word gets out you're seeing a psychologist,
Suddenly everyone thinks you're a basket case.

BETH: I understand.
Wanna talk about it?

CHRIS: Here's the deal: last year, I was involved in an
incident…
I wasn't directly involved. But I saw the whole thing.
I can't get into the details. Suffice it to say, there was a
review…
Final word was, the incident was in policy.

Deputy issued a command, suspect didn't comply,
deputy attempted to arrest the suspect.
Suspect resisted arrest, deputy applied reasonable
force, But suspect was unintentionally injured, and…
acquired a permanent disability.
Thing is… And I can't get into the details, but…
Well, put it this way: when this stuff happens,
you're not supposed to work out the story with the
other deputies.
But, of course, we do talk. We talk among ourselves,
we talk with legal counsel and the union rep…
And that's how you end up with certain…
adjustments. To the story.
But what if I told you, the deputy used the N word?
What if I told you, he has been doing it *for years?*
What if I told you, he's in a fucking gang?
Do you know what I'm talking about?

BETH: I think so.

CHRIS: What do you know?

BETH: The Sheriff Department has gangs.
Regulators, Executioners, Grim Reapers…a bunch
more.

CHRIS: It's not as bad as it sounds, but…
Whatever. I mean, look—I'm no snowflake.
Truth is, we deal with maniacs every fucking day.
Sometimes you have a split second to decide whether
to use force.
If you don't use it, the bad guy might.
So, shit happens.
No one in the world's going to make the right decision
a hundred percent of the time.
No genius, no saint, and certainly no judge or lawyer.
Shit is going to happen—*period.*

But sometimes…sometimes it really didn't need to
happen.
Sometimes it's just fucked up.

BETH: And how are you feeling about that?

CHRIS: Not great. You know? Not great…
It's an impossible situation.

BETH: How so?

CHRIS: I mean, I can either say what I got to say,
and destroy another cop's life…
Or I can keep my mouth shut, and let this eat away at
me.
Either way, I'm fucked.

BETH: One way seems like the right thing, though.

CHRIS: I'd be a snitch. A traitor. Total pariah.
My family could be in danger.
(Yelling to someone else now:)
No one… To myself.
In a minute! Alright, alright…
(To BETH)
I gotta go.

BETH: Can I—

CHRIS: I don't think so.
(He hangs up.)

(BETH takes the next call. LAURA. Again)

BETH: Hello, this is Beth.

*(Silence. Except for the same piece of classical music from
before.)*

BETH: Hello?

LAURA: How are you?

*(And now we see LAURA. She's not exactly BETH's age, and
doesn't necessarily have a physical resemblance. But there's*

something about her that somehow mirrors BETH—*could be the clothing, the lighting, the posture… Something.)*

BETH: I'm good, thanks… How are you?

LAURA: Busy night?

BETH: They always are…

LAURA: Is that right.

BETH: Pretty much… In fact, it's busier than ever.

LAURA: More calls.

BETH: Yes.

LAURA: How long have you been doing this?

BETH: A few years.

LAURA: What's your deal? If you don't mind my asking.

BETH: My deal?

LAURA: This is supposed to be a peer-based line, right? What do you call it, peer mentorship?

BETH: Yes.

LAURA: Kind of like AA.

BETH: Right.

LAURA: So, you're supposed to have lived experience.

BETH: Right…

LAURA: That's what I thought.
So, what's the experience?

BETH: Oh…well…

LAURA: You need more time?

BETH: No, it's just… It's unusual for me to be asked. Feels a bit like a job interview.

LAURA: Maybe it is.

BETH: What do you mean?

LAURA: I'm sorry if I made you uncomfortable.

BETH: No, it's fine…

LAURA: I used to teach sociology. We ask a lot of questions.

BETH: Well, I'm not supposed to go into personal details… That's against policy.
I will tell you this: I've done more than my share of drinking and drugging.
And I've been in jail.

LAURA: Have you.

BETH: Unfortunately, yeah… Not for a long time. But I have a rap sheet.
It would probably scare off a few neighbors, if they knew about it.

LAURA: So, now you're trying to share the wisdom.

BETH: I don't know that I have much wisdom, but… Something like that.

LAURA: Is it hard? I don't mean difficult. I mean… you know what I mean.

BETH: Yes. Sometimes.

LAURA: What's the hardest thing about it?

BETH: I guess when the caller hangs up.
Not always. But sometimes you just wanted to keep talking, and you can't call back, so…you just wonder. Did I upset them? Did I fail them?

LAURA: But they were already hurting.

BETH: Yes.

LAURA: So it was already hard.

BETH: Yes.

LAURA: Does it make you cry?

BETH: Sometimes. But the fact is…I'm just hearing their stories. They're the ones living them. So for me to cry feels like…I don't know. A kind of self- indulgence. It isn't about me. I'm just here to listen.

LAURA: Does it work?

BETH: I hope so.

LAURA: They either kill themselves or they don't.

(BETH *is alarmed.*)

BETH: That's…not the only reason people call.

LAURA: What else?

BETH: Anxiety… Boredom… Can't sleep… Loneliness, of course.

LAURA: It is amazing, isn't it? How we crammed so many people into giant cities, connected every one to the entire planet…
And everyone is lonelier than ever.
What else?

BETH: Well…sometimes it's just to let me know how they're doing.
If we spoke before.
Sometimes it's pranks, or…
We call them *strokers*.

LAURA: Does that mean what I think it means?

BETH: Yep.

LAURA: You're serious… People call a helpline to masturbate.

BETH: I'm afraid so.

LAURA: Jesus.
Is it a common occurrence?

BETH: More than you'd think.

LAURA: Kinda makes you despair about the human race.

BETH: It's pretty messed up.

LAURA: Well…that's not why I'm calling.

BETH: Good.

LAURA: Don't be so sure.
Are you gonna ask me? Why I'm calling?

BETH: I…usually don't.

LAURA: Why not?

BETH: It tends to come out on its own. I may ask: *How can I help.*

LAURA: Uh-huh.
I was a professor.
They kicked me out.

BETH: What happened?

LAURA: They said I was traumatizing the students.

BETH: Traumatizing them how?

LAURA: By telling them the truth.

BETH: About…?

LAURA: About their lives.
I'm not a good liar.
I'm not gonna tell them, *You'll be fine,*
When the truth is, the degree will not get 'em a job,
And they'll still be in debt fifteen years from now,
And most of them won't be able to afford a house, or
a child, And none of it matters anyway because the
planet is fucked.
By the way, it's not like I said all that.
I just told them they will have problems.
Problems that might not be solvable.
Which is just a fact.
It's not like I want them to despair.

BETH: And then what happened?

LAURA: Someone complains… Dean calls me in…
He tells me it's wrong of me to impose my politics on
student.
My politics… You believe that shit?
He never liked me. Had it in for me from minute one.
So I told him to get the fuck off my back.
But he kept talking… And I just…*snapped*.
I punched him in the mouth.
I ended up getting fired.

BETH: Damn…

LAURA: It was pretty bad timing.
My divorce had just been finalized.
Part of the reason I was at the end of my rope.
So, here I am, twice discarded…
Unemployed and divorced.
No children. No savings. No friends, really.
It's pretty grim.
I don't have an urge to kill myself. I'm just looking at it
objectively.

BETH: I…understand how you feel…

LAURA: But it's not about feelings. It's about a rational
outlook.
Are you a religious person?

BETH: Not in the conventional sense.

LAURA: What does that mean?

BETH: Well, I don't worship. I don't take religion
literally.
But I guess…I embrace the mystery.
I find certitude boring.
That includes the certitude that God doesn't exist.

LAURA: Well, if there's a God, he's a real piece of work,
don't you think?

I'm not talking about me now. That's trivial. I'm
talking about the world.

BETH: I…can see that perspective.

LAURA: I used to believe in God…
Over the years he just started to look so…incompetent.
I mean, it's either incompetent or evil, right?
Allowing so much… wrongness.

BETH: Except…

LAURA: What?

BETH: Well… Isn't a universe where wrong things can
happen the only possible moral universe?

LAURA: You could reverse that.
Isn't a universe where wrong things are routine
fundamentally immoral?

BETH: Moral choice still exists.

LAURA: No one chooses to suffer.
It's random, and meaningless, and fucking inevitable.

BETH: But isn't suffering just the other side of
happiness?
Isn't loss just the other side of love?
You could say that loss is the exact measure of love.
You could say suffering makes happiness possible.

LAURA: Or you could say it makes it a fraud.
Anyway, like I said—I look at it as a practical
question…
Sometimes, the energy required to live simply exceeds
the benefit.
The truth is, there is no rational argument against
ending your life.

BETH: I'm not sure about that.

LAURA: Well, think: why do religious people object to
it?

BETH: They consider it a sin.

LAURA: And yet they worship martyrs. You can argue
Jesus killed himself.
He could have stopped it any moment.
But all ancient Christians, really…they courted death,
because they believed real life comes after.
So they would dare the Romans to kill them.
It was like suicide by cop, on a mass scale.
Then they became the dominant religion.
The priests realized they'd better start condemning
suicide, or Christianity would become a giant death
cult. And they would all be expected to die horribly.

BETH: Religious people are not the only ones who
oppose suicide.

LAURA: The secular argument just replaced sin with
crime. It's still a fallacy. Because if you can be victim
and culprit at the same time, the concept of crime
doesn't make any sense. The only way that taking your
life can be considered criminal, or even unethical, is if
one assumes that the life you're taking is not actually
yours. It belong to God, to the king, to society. To your
parents, your children… The ones you're working for.
Responsible for.
But if I am not mine, is there such thing as *I*?
In fact—that train of thought just ends up validating
suicide. 'Cause the only way to claim your life as yours
is to actually…*take it.*
I don't necessarily want to claim anything, by the way.
I'm just suggesting there's no rational argument
against killing yourself.

BETH: That's…still not an argument for it.

LAURA: You don't need an argument for it.
Just the realization that you don't want to do this
anymore.
You don't even know how to do it.

And it happened over a long time, day by day,
without drums and trumpets…
The unhappiness just crept up on you, like a shadow,
ever so slowly.
Until every corner of your life was in the dark.
And your whole life started feeling like a pantomime.
You play the part, stick to the script… You smile when
you're smiled to.
But eventually you can't help catching yourself.
This person.
This character.
It's not you.
It never was.
Someone else wrote it. You were just cast in the role,
without even asking for it, and the costume got stuck
to your skin.
And you just want to rip it off, the costume, the mask…
But underneath is just another mask.
Because the unhappiness is always ashamed of itself.

BETH: I understand.

LAURA: Do you.

BETH: I think so.

LAURA: So, you agree.

BETH: I didn't say that.

LAURA: Well… Give me a reason.

BETH: Do you need one now?

LAURA: What do you think?

BETH: I'm sorry… Let me ask this directly.
Did you make a plan to end your life?

LAURA: Oh, boy… Did I ever.

BETH: Today?

LAURA: Why not?

BETH: I mean, have you taken any steps—

LAURA: Stop. I know the drill. Let me save you the
time—I'm not gonna call anyone else.
Especially not a place that's gonna trace my call, and
send someone here.
So let's just keep this hypothetical.
Maybe I did, maybe I didn't.
But *if* I did.
What would you tell me?

BETH: I would urge you to call—

LAURA: I'm asking *you*. What reason would *you* give
me?

(BETH *hesitates.*)

LAURA: Tick. Tock.

BETH: I guess I'd just say… That everything means
something. That maybe—

LAURA: *(Laughs)* Everything means something?
Now that's a self-contradicting statement…
'Cause it doesn't actually mean anything!

BETH: I'm just trying to say… Whatever you care
about—a friend, a pet…

LAURA: I have neither.

BETH: Politics, then. Art. Yoga. Food. Whatever it is:
It means something. It's worth something.
Whether it's inherently worthy, or made worthy
by your investment, your act of caring, That can be
debated—the point is: if that thing has value, *Life* does.

LAURA: The earth will burst into flames.
Cities will turn to ashes, or be swept away by oceans.
Civilization will tumble into darkness.
It's *when*, not *if*.

BETH: Well…you obviously care about that.
So that's one thing.

LAURA: One thing I can do nothing about.
The entire human race has *already* committed suicide.
The poison is working its way through the system.
Some people just don't know it yet.

BETH: Maybe… Maybe it is when, not if.
But isn't two thousand years better than a hundred?

LAURA: To be honest, I'm not sure.
You wanna hear a story?

BETH: Yeah.

LAURA: There was this man, a friend of a friend…
His name was…Tom. He lived alone.
Apparently he had developed a ritual: when he felt
down, he would fix himself a drink and take out his
revolver. Then he would sip his drink, and think of
all the reasons he had to NOT kill himself. For every
reason he could think of, he would take out a bullet,
until the drum was empty, then go to bed, and reload
the gun in the morning.
And he did that for years.
Until he ran out of reasons.

(BETH *takes this in.*)

LAURA: There is no free will. It's an illusion.
Every choice has already been made.
Everything we think, everything we feel, everything
we do is baked in.
We behave in the exact way we're meant to.
I know this sounds dispiriting.
The irony is that we are programmed to hate the idea
that we're programmed.
To preserve the illusion that we master our destiny,
That we earn our fortune, that we can deserve
happiness.

We master *nothing.*
Fortune is random.
Assholes are happy, good people are miserable.
There's no rhyme, there's no reason, there's no God's
plan, and there's no fucking escape.
Other than…you know.
Escape.

BETH: Laura…

LAURA: What?

BETH: You asked what my deal was.

LAURA: I did.

BETH: My answer was evasive.

LAURA: How so?

BETH: It's weird—keeping a secret is a burden…
Being forced to talk about it is just as bad.
I find that the only freedom I can enjoy in the matter,
Is to sometimes volunteer the information, and
sometimes withhold it.

LAURA: The suspense builds.

BETH: My stepbrother killed himself five years ago.
He was twenty-five.
I didn't call him back that night.
He tried me a few times…
I just turned the phone off.

LAURA: Did he use to call a lot?

BETH: There were periods when he would call every
day.
It was pretty hard.
He was chronically depressed, and…
We had a difficult relationship.
We grew up in a bad family environment.
Thing is, my stepfather…
(A long exhale)

LAURA: I understand.

BETH: It's more complicated than that.
You see…my stepbrother looked just like him.
He even sounded like him.
So, when he grew up, dealing with him…
it brought everything back.
And not dealing with him was a relief.

LAURA: So, now you talk to other people.
Because you didn't take that call.

BETH: That's part of it.

LAURA: Go on.

BETH: I…struggled with depression myself.
If your own parent doesn't love you, if you're just an
object to him…
How unlovable must you be?
So I fell into drugs, and fucked-up relationships…
And then the guilt.
What I'm trying to say is…I was there.
I ran out of reasons.
I didn't have a plan.
I was just…gonna let it happen, I guess.
I thought I was bound to overdose, or to drown,
or get run over by a truck.
I just didn't care.
And then, one day, I ran into this old guy, walking an
old dog…
He passed me by, and I heard the dog barking,
and I saw that the man had fallen.
I helped him up, and I walked him home.
He invited me inside, offered to make me a cup of tea.
I said, no thanks.
He insisted.
His name was Jacob.
He's dead now.
He lived in this small house, and the house was stuffy,

like your typical old man house…
But it was extraordinary.
Books and paintings and strange objects from all over
the world.
There was a framed Emperor scorpion from Africa.
Hand-blown glass from Venice.
An ancient chess set from Russia.
The man had been everywhere—
first with the Navy, then the merchant marine…
Anyway, he started telling me all these amazing
stories, and…
I came back the next day.
To hear more stories.
And after a while, I realized…
I had a reason.
And then I kept finding more.

(A beat)

LAURA: Beth, you said— Yes?

BETH: Yes.

LAURA: Short for Elizabeth, I suppose.

BETH: Sure.

LAURA: You don't sound sure.

BETH: It's…actually not my real name.

LAURA: Why do you use a fake name?

BETH: It's mainly a privacy thing…
But also, we are supposed to keep the job separate.
As a way to reduce the stress.
If I do this under a different name, it's supposed to
help.

LAURA: Does it?

BETH: Not much.

LAURA: So, what keeps you coming back?

BETH: I suppose…when I'm on a shift, I'm focused.
I'm not multi-tasking. I'm not running through my to-do list.
I'm a hundred percent focused on the person I'm speaking to, and…I don't know.
I *care*.

LAURA: I can see that…

BETH: Know something?

LAURA: What's that?

BETH: I have a feeling you would be very good at this.

LAURA: That might be the funniest thing I ever heard.

BETH: I mean it.

LAURA: You're serious… You think I should be hosting the Lonely Hearts Club.

BETH: Well, I don't call it that, but… Yeah.
It's an interesting club, you know. All kinds of people.

LAURA: Loneliness is a big slut.

BETH: Yes. I think I'm gonna steal that.

LAURA: Be my guest.

BETH: It's *Maggie,* by the way.

LAURA: Oh.
I kinda liked Beth.

BETH: I know, right? Me too.

LAURA: Well… This has been an interesting talk.
Goodnight, M—

BETH: Wait…

LAURA: No.
Not tonight.
Shit, I'd probably botch it now…
Nothing more pathetic than a failed suicide attempt.

And then having to tell yourself, Don't give up… Try again!

I'm joking.

BETH: Yes… Okay. Good. Good. Please call anytime, if…

Or for any reason. Anything at all.

Just ask for Beth.

LAURA: I might do that.

Goodnight, Beth.

BETH: Goodnight.

(LAURA *hangs up.* BETH *checks the time. Opens the curtains. First light of day.*)

(*She paces, drinks some water. She puts the headset back on. Before she can hit any key:*)

CORINNE: Can't even take a break

CHRIS: It's an impossible situation

MICHAEL: You don't know what's coming from behind that rock

SHARON: I have snakes for bones

LAURA: Maybe I did, maybe I didn't

ANDY: You can't fucking whistle for it

ELLIS: I would have bled for her

JINX: Fuck that shit

RUBY: So fucking pathetic

RAY: I know how they would look like dead

ELLIS: The rejection, the contempt

LAURA: The earth will burst into flames—

(BETH *takes out the ear pods. She catches her breath. Calms down.*)

(*She tries again… All quiet now. She hits a key—next call.*)

SHARON: Beth?

BETH: Yeah?

SHARON: It's Sharon. From earlier?

BETH: Yes… Hi, Sharon.

SHARON: I wrote one.
A song. Or a poem. Whatever.

BETH: Right…

SHARON: It's not finished, but I wanted to get you
before your shift ends… Is that okay?

BETH: Sure.

SHARON: You ready? Okay, here it is: Illusion -
delusion…
(She stops. Suddenly shy. She clears her throat and resumes:
rapid fire)
Illusion—delusion—confusion
Draw your freakin' conclusion
They feed you conspiracies
They prey on your miseries
They rewrite history
Make their crimes mysteries
The secret keepers
The promise breakers
The fake believers
The silent takers
They call your fight treason
They call their lies reason
It's all a mind prison
Can't trust your own eyes
Can't tell truth from lies
Chem trails in the sky
Crisis actors on site
Their smiles, more lies
They're knives in disguise

Another day dies
Another night cries
All you got is your rage
All you got is this song
All you got is a cage
All you got is a a bomb
All you are is alone
Cuz your head is all wrong
But your heart is still strong
And the light is still on
No one has very long
Keep on writing this song…
That's how far I got.
I don't know. Maybe it is finished.

BETH: It's…amazing.

SHARON: You think so?

BETH: I really do.
SHARON: Thank you.

BETH: Thank you.

SHARON: I'll let you go now.

BETH: I can stay… It's not a problem.

SHARON: No no no… You got better things to do.

Have a great day.

BETH: You too.

(BETH *checks the time…this is it. End of shift. She puts the computer to sleep, then dials a number on her smart phone: the first time we see her make a call. And this time we don't hear the other side at all. Could be a friend, a relative, a past or present love interest… We just don't know.*)

BETH: Hey… Good morning. I didn't wake you, did I?
Yeah, no—I know you wake up early— That's why…

Nothing, I…I was just wondering if you wanna get some breakfast.

Maybe that place you mentioned, what's it called?

Oh.

No no no—no problem… It was just a spur of the moment thing.

No worries. I understand.

Yes, absolutely…some other time.

You too…

Bye bye.

(BETH *reaches for a cigarette. Sticks in her mouth. Grabs the gas lighter, brings it up…*)

(*…then throws the cigarette in the trash.*)

(*She throws out the coffee filter with the old coffee grounds, puts a new filter in, fills it with ground coffee and fills the tank from a pitcher. She flips the switch back on.*)

(*She looks at the vase of flowers. The flowers look tired. There's some water left in the pitcher, so she pours into the vase. She sits and waits for the coffee.*)

(*A garbage truck beeps.*)

(*The pot starts gurgling.*)

(*Light spills through the window.*)

END OF PLAY